AN INTRODUCTION TO

PLAYING SONATINAS

A FIRST REPERTORY FOR EARLY-GRADE PIANISTS
SELECTED AND EDITED BY
DENES AGAY

CONTENTS

This book Copyright © 1995 by Yorktown Music Press, Inc.

T0087897

SONATA AND SONATINA

Sonata and sonatina are essentially identical musical forms. The sonatina is a "little sonata" usually shorter and easier to perform than a sonata. The word "sonata" comes from the Italian *sonare*, "to sound," and originally it meant merely a "sound piece," (a musical thought sounded on one or more instruments). In its early form it was a composition of two or three distinct, thematically related sections on the pattern of A-B, or A-B-A. As developed by the classical masters (Haydn, Mozart, and Beethoven). It became a larger, extended, and unified musical structure built on two or three contrasting themes, presented in a continuous melodic flow in related keys with connecting transitional passages. This structure usually referred to as "sonata-allegro" form or "first movement" form, consists of three sections:

Exposition: contains the main theme, a second theme in a related key (usually the dominant), and often also a closing theme.

Development: contains one or more previously presented themes or theme fragments "developed" into varied new sound patterns, moving freely through new keys and leading directly into the recapitulation.

Recapitulation: which is a repetition of the exposition section, with all themes in the original key.

The **sonatina** does not always contain all the components of the sonata form. In its simplest examples it is a small three-part song form (A-B-A) with the melodies simply stated, without thematic expansions and developments.

    Sonatas, and often sonatinas too, usually consist of two to four independent, self-contained parts called *movements*. The second movement can be simple two- or three-part song form and the last movement is usually a rondo.

Rondo: musical form in which a main theme or section alternates with one or more secondary themes, called *episodes.*In its simplest form, the rondo is very close to the ternary form of a A-B-A pattern. More often the rondo consists of a main theme and two episodes (pattern A-B-A-C-A).

Binary Form: also called "two-part song form," consists of two sections (two musical sentences), A and B, both of which are usually repeated.

"Rounded"
Binary Form: when the second section of the binary form concludes with a restatement of the first section in whole or in part

Ternary Form: "three-part song form," pattern A-B-A or A-B-C.

Sonatina on Five Notes

I.

Allegretto

Oscar Bolck
(1839–1888)

* *2nd Theme reversed.*

II.
(Three-part song form)

Moderato

III.
(Rondo)

Vivace

*Episode reversed.

Little Sonata

I.

("Rounded" binary form)

C. H. Wilton
(18th Century)

II.
Minuetto
("Rounded" binary form)

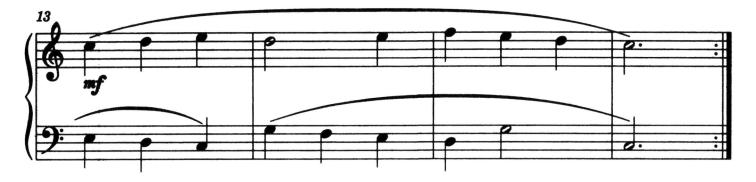

Early English Sonatina

(Ternary form)

William Duncombe
(18th Century)

Song Sonatina
(Ternary form)

Cornelius Gurlitt
(1820–1901)

Sonatinetta

I.

("Rounded" binary form)

Denes Agay
(1911–)

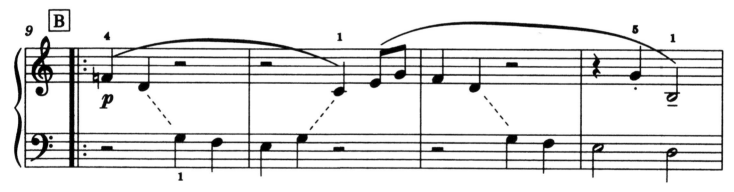

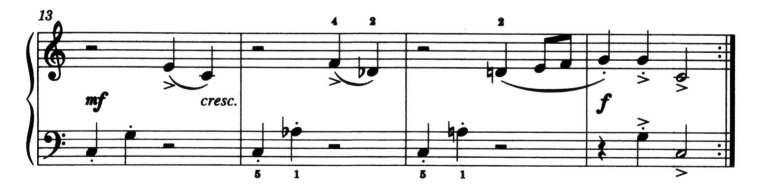

II.
Little Song Without Words
(Binary form)

III.

(Ternary form*)

* *Can also be regarded as a Rondo,*
in its simplest form.

Hungarian Sonatina

I.

("Rounded" binary form)

Kalmán Chován
(1852–1928)

II.
(Ternary form)

III.
(Ternary form)

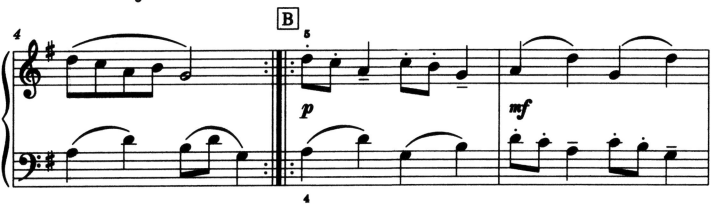

Petite Sonatine
On 18th Century French Dance Melodies
I.

(Binary form)

Denes Agay
(1911–   )

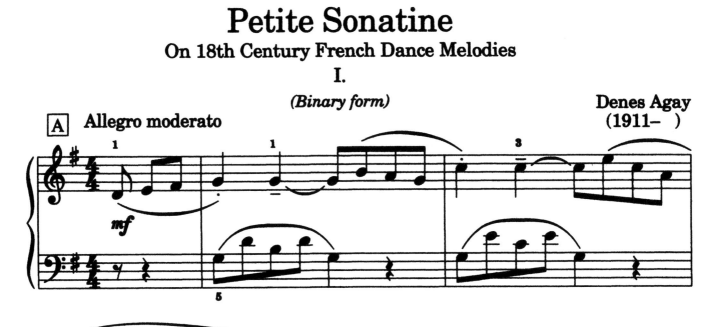

B2 *(in varied form)*

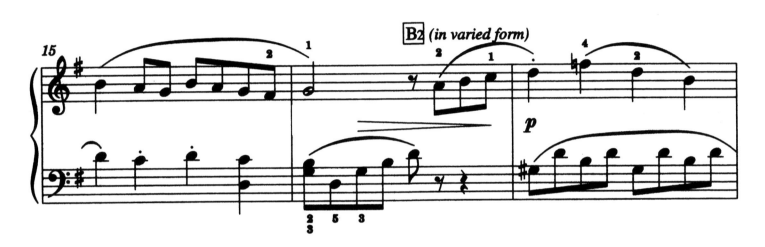

II.
Ballade
("Rounded" binary form)

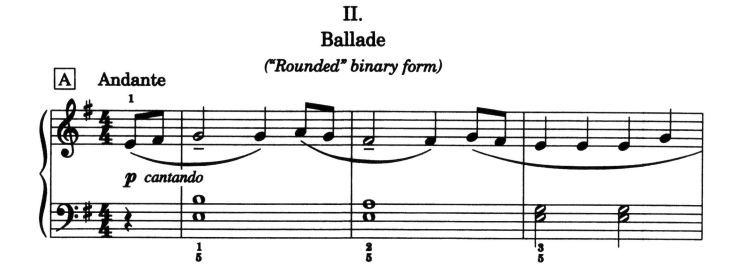

III.
Contredanse
(Ternary form)

Sonata No. 2

(1st Movement)

Jean T. Latour
(1766–1837)

Recital Sonatina

I.

Denes Agay
(1911–   )

5

1st Theme (Recap.)

Extension

II.

("Rounded" binary form)

Andante cantabile

III.
Rondo–Valse

(Play: Theme-Episode I-Theme-Episode II-Theme-Coda)

Moderato

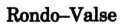

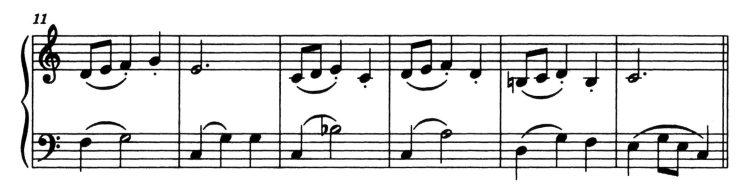

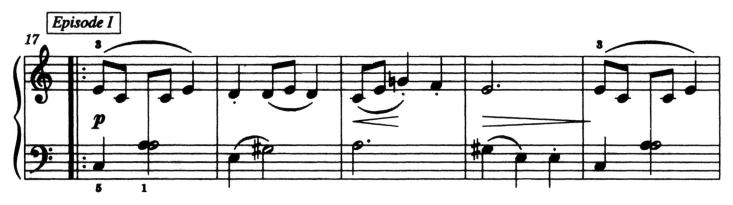

Episode II

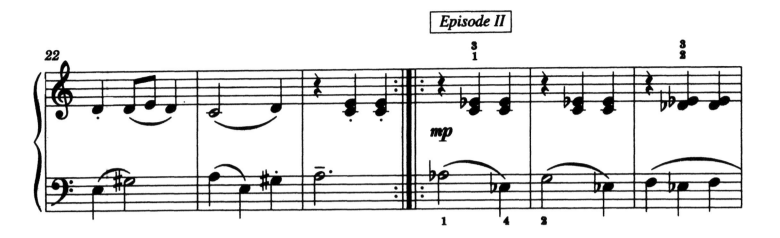

Coda

Early American Sonatina

(Ternary form)

Benjamin Carr
(1768–1831)

Sonatina in G

Daniel Gottlob Türk
(1756–1813)

Finale

D.C.

Repeat Finale till sign (⊕)
then play Coda.

Dance Sonatina

Denes Agay
(1911–   )

I.

II.
Mini–Waltz
("Rounded" binary form)

III.
Polka Rondolette

Giocoso

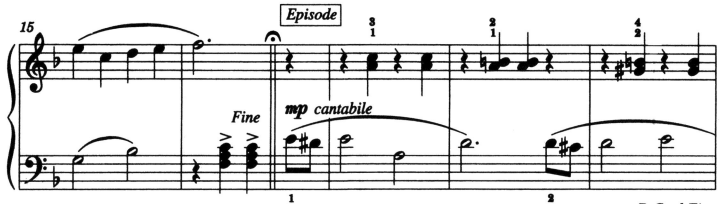